The Parent's Dictionary

The Parent's Dictionary

from Arrrrgggggh!
to Zzzzzzzzzz . . .

MERRILL FURMAN
Illustrated by Ed Morrow

ℭℬ
CONTEMPORARY
BOOKS
A TRIBUNE NEW MEDIA COMPANY

Library of Congress Cataloging-in-Publication Data

Furman, Merrill.
    The parent's dictionary : from Arrrrgggggh! to
Zzzzzzzzzzzz— / Merrill Furman ; illustrated by Ed
Morrow.
      p.   cm.
   ISBN 0-8092-3512-9
   1. Child rearing—Humor.   2. Parents—
Humor.   I. Title.
PN6231.C315F87   1995
818′.5402—dc20   94-45349
                           CIP

Copyright © 1995 by Merrill Furman
Illustrations copyright © 1995 by Ed Morrow
All rights reserved
Published by Contemporary Books, Inc.
Two Prudential Plaza, Chicago, Illinois 60601-6790
Manufactured in the United States of America
International Standard Book Number: 0-8092-3512-9
10 9 8 7 6 5 4 3 2 1

For my parents and Jordan

Acknowledgments

My special thanks go to Marc Furman, Robin Fine-Furman, Ed Friedman, Judi Smolanoff, Ed Morrow, Janet Rosen, Michael Furman, Victoria Satterthwaite, Gene Brissie, and my agent, Sheree Bykofsky.

Thanks to my cat, Blanche DuBois, who served as paperweight. And thanks to Michael Serdikoff, who rescued this book when my computer crashed twenty days before deadline.

A

action figures
Kids on chocolate.

after-school program
Where the *real* learning takes place.

age-appropriate
Meets the needs of a preset category. As with the Nielsen ratings, someone other than you has helped set the norm.

allowance
The timely payment of extortion money.

alphabetical order
The reason your kid is behind the same kid all through school.

amniotic fluid
The popcorn packing around baby.

amusement park
Where the combination of corn dogs, cotton candy, and Tilt-A-Whirl is deadly.

ancestors
Those who raised children before you and did not survive.

ant farm
Solution to child's desire for a dog.

"Are we there yet?"
Words repeated at five-mile intervals, accompanied by seat banging, in a car.

A-student
The one your kid terrorizes.

attention span

> The time it takes your child to forget what you've just said.

au pair

> A welcome addition to the family that doesn't make mother's ankles swell or give her heartburn.

average student

> About medium height and build.

B

baby
> Starter person.

baby announcement
> "I gotta pee!"

baby bonnet
> Cradle cap.

baby bottle
> Generic breast milk.

Baby Bottle

baby experts

Those who stop you in the supermarket to give advice.

baby fat

What takes mom *forever* to lose.

baby food

Eaten when there's no teeth—at the beginning and end of life.

baby leash
Device that enables child to pull parent's chain.

baby monitor
Parent beeper.

baby names
Great-Aunt Bertha immortalized.

baby rocker
Raffi.

Baby Food

baby shower
Kid in sink with duck.

baby steps
Those taken outside baby's room when baby's asleep.

baby talk
Tyke-o-babble.

baby wipes
In tandem with diapers, parent will go through, say, about a million of these. They're used for everything from wiping messy rear ends to cleaning linoleum. In a pinch, they can put a shine on hubcaps. One box will last an hour.

back-to-school night

Parents in those tiny seats with their knees around their ears.

Band-Aids

Fashion wear for three-year-olds. Injury's not a prerequisite.

Barbie Dream House

Barbie, Midge, and Skipper welcome Ken and his friends in rooms done in pink and lavender. The closets are full of little spike shoes and cheap, sleazy teddies. Forget it, Barb. That wedding dress is a pipe dream.

bath time

The call to bathe is, for some children, like an air-raid signal. Little bodies will scurry under the nearest bed until the threat of soap and water disappears. Parents must pull child out by extremities while being careful not to wedge head, somehow grown larger, between bed frame and floor. Child, at no time, will cooperate.

"Because I said so"

Parent grasping at straws.

bed

A kid's trampoline.

bedtime

What Saddam may have meant when he referred to the "mother of all battles."

bedtime story

That which puts parent to sleep before child.

belching

Universal kid language.

between-meal snacks

Food that, for some children, constitutes major daily intake.

Bedtime

bib
The thing that the food misses.

bickering
Communication between siblings.

big wheels
Family minivan.

birth certificate
Deed to baby.

birthright

Two pushes and he's out!

biting

Act in which child applies new teeth to any skin surface other than his own.

blended family

Hard to manage, but then your old-fashioned unblended family didn't get along, either.

bloodstains

Road maps of your child's activities.

Bib

blue

Primary color child turns when upset.

board games

How parent feels after two hours of Candy Land—bored with games.

bonding

Occurs when unsuspecting parent finds child's uncapped Whacky Glue.

boo-boo

Comforting term for laceration requiring twelve stitches.

book smarts
The sixty-dollar price of a college textbook.

braces
Robo-chops.

"Brady Bunch"
The reason the Brady bill was passed—to protect people like these.

breakfast
Sugarfest.

breast-feeding

The original Happy Meal.

breast pump

Like pump shoes, a size smaller than the woman wears. Unlike pumps, they don't come in navy.

bribe

That which is offered to child in exchange for what she should be doing anyway.

brushing teeth

Child lets water run for three minutes while making faces in mirror.

"But, Ma . . ."
How child starts 33 percent of sentences.

buying in bulk
When a pregnant woman shops.

C

cabin fever
Homesickness.

Caesarean section
Baby born near Naples.

camp food

Terrible food child would never eat at home but is happy to eat when at camp.

camp laundry

What parent throws out at the end of summer.

car pool

Junior left the window down in mom's Mercedes. And it rained.

car seat

Spot from which child screams, "Get me out of here!"

caregiver

A modern term for *baby-sitter*, this person does for child what you cannot because you're off somewhere working to make the money to afford a caregiver.

cereal box

Kids' morning paper.

change of clothes

Needed by parent, who is likely to be soiled in some way while feeding, burping, or diaper-changing child.

Caregiver

cheating

Child copying off another child's paper. Some kids even copy the name—always a giveaway!

child authority

The older kid on the block.

child labor

Kid forced to make bed.

child psychologist

Any four-year-old.

Child Psychologist

childbirth classes

Where *The Miracle of Birth* is shown to dads with weak stomachs.

children

People who wield power disproportionate to their size.

child-sized

Little stuff that costs as much as big stuff.

choke foods

Those that clog the windpipe en route to the arteries.

class bully

Child who brings out killer instinct in parent.

Cliffs Notes

Child "reads" *Hamlet* in fifteen minutes, has rest of evening free.

college

The four-year period when parents are permitted access to the telephone.

comic books

Literature for reluctant readers.

Children

commercials

Sixty seconds that precede "Mom, can I have . . . ?"

company

People who overstimulate your child—then go.

contact sports

Those that require a trip to the emergency room.

cranky

Used to describe parent whose child missed a nap.

crib

Place where child's stuffed animals sleep at night.

crossing guard

The blind octogenarian who helps your child across the busy highway.

curfew

Hour by which child must be home and accounted for. If curfew is missed, child may be grounded according to whim of parent. When child's room contains CD player, Nintendo, and telephone, impact of punishment is somewhat diminished.

curriculum

> Statement of what child will be taught—not necessarily what he will know.

D

dating

> Activity that is staunchly objected to by child—when engaged in by single parent.

day camp

> Where kids learn to make fart sounds with their armpits.

Day Camp

33

Dessert

delayed gratification

When parent puts off own needs for eighteen years.

dessert

What kids think they're entitled to after eating one measly pea.

detention

Validation from another person that your child is a handful.

diaper

A garment that must be applied while child is doing half-gainers off changing table.

Diaper

diaper bag
A mom's pocketbook.

diaper pail
Dump site.

diaphragm
That which, had it been used, would have kept parent from needing this book. Check for holes.

diary
Notes for "Oprah."

dinner hour
> Time of day that conflicts with soccer practice.

Disneyland
> A kid's Vegas.

distant relative
> Too far to baby-sit.

Dr. Spock
> Vulcan physician.

doctor's office

Place where new germs are acquired.

"Don't touch!"

Phrase that induces hearing loss in children.

drugs

The self-medication of parent to deal with
stress and burnout.

due date

Expiration date on womb.

Doctor's Office

dysfunctional
>   The modern family.

E

earache
>   Pain that occurs only in the middle of the
>   night.

early admission
>   Child confesses quickly to something she did.

Educational Toys

early dismissal

When kids get a head start on wrecking the house.

"Eat your vegetables"

Kids wonder, "Do potato chips count?"

educational toys

Toys that supposedly have a higher play value than regular toys. Toy for toy, however, it is still the Styrofoam packing and cardboard box that get the most action.

effective parenting

That which, after the twelfth round, leaves parent still standing.

emergency numbers

Police station, fire department, and places that deliver.

empty nest

The calm before the grandchildren.

essay

Child stretches a single thought over twelve pages.

"Everybody else's parents . . ."
Child thinking he got saddled with losers.

exchange student
Parent wonders, "Can we keep her instead?"

expecting
Parent waiting for an apology.

explaining death
Why camphor flakes should not be fed to goldfish.

Explaining Death

extended family

Those you move away from at the first opportunity.

extra-absorbent

Child's brain when it comes to batting averages and song lyrics. Leaky on other subjects.

F

facts of life

Fact 1: Parents want to avoid the stork question as long as possible. Fact 2: Kids have pretty much heard what's going on by the time parents get to it.

Extended Family

fairy tale

Parent's account of her own past to child, in which she never cut school, went below the waist, or tried drugs.

family crisis

Running out of toilet paper.

family heirloom

Valued keepsake considered junk by child who will acquire it.

family jewels

Your children.

family name

In today's family, may include mother's maiden name, her child's paternal surname, stepfather's last name, and *his* kid's hyphenated mom-dad name. Tough on the mail carrier.

family pet

Creature with a short shelf life.

family planning

Children spaced apart for maximum emotional growth. If planning a large family, with births at three-year intervals, mom will be pregnant or changing diapers for eighteen years. You call this a plan?

Facts of Life

Fairy Tale

family plot
Hamsters in shoe boxes out back.

family reunion
This is an opportunity to see cousins and intermarry, thereby creating some of the insanity that later shows up in FAMILY TREE.

family room
Dominated by whoever has the remote control.

family tree
On which is hung oddballs, lunatics, and fools, invariably attributed to "the other side of the family."

Family Pet

family vacation

When family members can't wait to get away from home but take as much of it with them as they can.

family values

Discounts that apply to groups of four or more.

fast food

What mom swore, when breast-feeding child, she would never give him. Now part of her survival kit.

Father's Day

A day when dad gets attention, respect, and gifts that have been charged to his credit card.

fear of abandonment

Fear of (finally) making it to the front of the (long) line at the supermarket and having your (newly potty trained) child suddenly shout, "I HAVE TO GO!" whereupon you must abandon your (loaded to capacity) shopping cart and lose your place.

fetal curl

Child's grasp around a candy bar.

fever

What the unprepared child gets on the day of an exam by holding thermometer under a hot light for five minutes.

field trip

Mom plans an outing—hairdresser, lunch, and shopping. No kids.

finals

Last chance to bring up that F.

finger food

Child makes no distinctions between Cheerios and spaghetti marinara.

first aid kit
A fifty-pound box of Band-Aids.

first aid manual
"Kiss the boo-boo."

first haircut
Traumatic experience for child, who will make a run for it when approached with scissors. Parents should position themselves at all exits.

first tooth
Jagged bump that provides endless months of child's screaming before surfacing.

first words

Likely to be *ba* and interpreted by parent in free fashion.

firstborn

The one who sees the shrink first.

flash card

Child showing parent a progress report that is less than satisfactory.

First Words

flextime

A new concept in the workplace whereby a parent may adjust her schedule to meet the needs of the family. Works well in theory; in reality, you bring home what didn't get done at the office.

food fight

Getting your child to try spinach.

food shopping

You go out for peanut butter, milk, and a loaf of bread. It takes fifteen minutes.

Food Shopping *with* the Kids

food shopping *with* the kids

You go out for peanut butter, milk, and a loaf of bread. You come back with Oreo cookies, twelve types of chips, and a splitting headache. It takes two hours.

formative years

The time when neuroses are shaped.

full-time parent

Person who gets asked, "What do you *do* all day?"

G

germs

What gets passed around when kids network.

golden rule

"Do as I say, not as I do."

graduation

Child has demonstrated minimal understanding of course material, which is sufficient to pass to next grade. The shock of this is celebrated with a formal ceremony and the award of a certificate that may be referred to by parent when in doubt of child's competence.

grandmother

Someone with *two* generations to worry about.

gross motor skills

Nose picking is one. Butt scratching is another.

growing pains

When parent realizes that expenses are growing faster than means.

growing up

First signs that parent will one day have the house back.

Growth Spurt

growth spurt

That which happens the day after you buy your child a whole new wardrobe. Perverse phenomenon that teaches the value of hand-me-downs.

guilt

That which is given freely but exacts a cost.

gym class

Ritual separation of the men from the boys. Establishes a pecking order that will haunt males into adulthood.

Gym Class

H

Halloween

Annual restocking of child's sugar supply.

Halloween costume

What child wears to bed for days before and after.

hand-eye coordination

Necessary for parent, who must write a lot of checks.

hands-on

Child grabbing.

having it all

An ulcer, a headache, and a nervous breakdown.

"He touched me!"

Child announcing that an elbow (knee, foot, etc.) brushed against her for a split second, causing a state of emergency.

hide-and-seek

Parent's keys last seen with baby.

Hide-and-Seek

high chair

One of the few times parent and child see eye-to-eye.

hobby

Activity parent enjoys that he no longer has time for.

home alone

Parent is at work, the kids are at school, and Fido's left unattended with a urinary problem.

home improvement

Child keeps bedroom door shut.

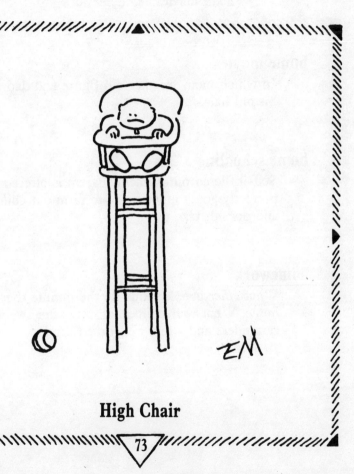

High Chair

73

home movies

In which mom sees her old figure and dad sees his old hair.

home schooling

Self-inflicted punishment. Parent is offered a perfectly good opportunity to farm out children and doesn't take it.

homework

What *other* people's kids do the minute they get home. What *your* child does only after twenty reminders and a few well-timed threats.

Hot Wheels

Any vehicle a 16-year-old is driving.

hunger alarm

What goes off in your child the moment you sit down to relax.

I

"I'm bored"

Complaint of child who can't find anything to do in a house full of merchandise.

imaginary friend

The reason for the extra place setting at the dinner table.

in crowd

Group that excludes beings of assumed lesser worth on grounds they would diminish aura that surrounds in crowd. Needless to say, your child is desperate to belong.

in utero

The last time mom has child's undivided attention.

inappropriate behavior

Parent changing stinky, voluminous diaper in full view of next table at a four-star restaurant.

inappropriate language

Parent asks child, "Where the #%*&@! did you learn to speak like that?"

infant swing

Lulls child into comalike state in which parent can subliminally suggest, "Keep sleeping. . . . keep sleeping. . . ."

Innocent

inheritance

What your kids can't wait to get their hands on—never mind that you must die first.

innocent

Child with hand in cookie jar who's got a good lawyer.

instant gratification

The hug and kiss your child gives you when you say "Yes."

IQ

Parent starts off knowing everything—winds up knowing nothing.

"It followed me home"

How the rabbit turned up in your kitchen. This version of events leaves out the food lure, the rope, and the tranquilizer darts.

J

Jack and Jill

Two unsupervised children who should have been outfitted with Medic Alert buttons.

juggling

A circus act, where moms are the real professionals.

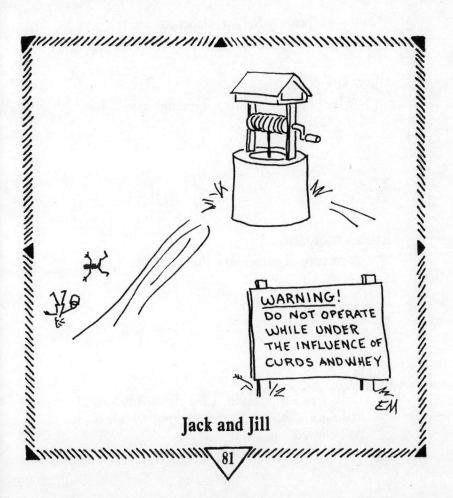

Jack and Jill

"Just say No"

After you've explained it enough times, just say "No!"

K

Kodak moment

A picture of somebody else's family.

L

labeling

Classification of child. Like the words *light* and *natural* on food products, not all labels can be believed.

lag time

The delay between when a parent asks a question and when the child answers it.

latchkey kids

Those who learn to use the microwave early on.

let down

What a dad feels when a nursing mom says, "They're just for the baby."

letter home from camp

Something child sends when he's upset that makes you feel rotten.

letting go

Child releases new balloon but didn't mean to.

"Like father, like son"

Depending on the similarities, mother is either delighted or ready to hang herself.

lullaby

Song whose violent, disturbed, and twisted lyrics are meant to soothe baby.

M

"Maaa-aaa-aaah!!!"
Child calling parent from two rooms away.

manipulatives
Dressed in fancy words, they're still toys.

maternal instinct
What mom wakes up with the day after seeing that plus sign.

maternity clothes
Sailor tops in XXXL.

medicine cabinet
What child raids for his doctor's kit.

middle child
The one who gets the hump in the backseat.

milk money
Thirty-five cents that goes for a candy bar.

"Mine!"
Child has exclusive property rights to everything within her sight and reach.

mobile
A suspended animation.

modern math
A calculator.

mombie
Mom without coffee.

mom's pockets
What child uses to carry his rock collection.

Mombie

morning sickness
Shake hands with Mr. Toilet.

Mother's Day
Day on which Mother's routine is not disturbed.

N

name-calling
Parent calls out every name in the house—including the dog's—until she finally spits out the right one.

Needles

natural childbirth
What happens once the drugs wear off.

needles
The "N" word. Children should be properly chloroformed before receiving.

nesting instinct
Fatal attraction to Pine Sol and a mop.

night before Christmas
When you can count on your kids to behave.

night-light
Four watts that provide emotional comfort.

9-1-1
Child pressing buttons on speed-dialer, looking for Grandma.

"No!"
No means yes and yes means yes to a kid.

"Now!"
Child's sense of when her needs should be met.

"No!"

nuclear family

Grouping that may explode due to mere proximity.

O

OB-GYN

Guy mom would recognize anywhere by the top of his head.

Oedipus complex

Freudian explanation of a son's early attachment to his mother. Resolved a few years later, when son tells his mom to walk five steps ahead and act as if she doesn't know him.

old age
Process accelerated by children.

on demand
A feeding schedule that sucks.

only child
One who gets as much attention as a crowd.

onosecond ("Oh, no" second)
The time it takes to realize that your child has gone to the bathroom—and you've just removed her diaper.

oppositional child
Future trial attorney.

other woman
The young girl wrapped around teenaged son on the living room couch.

"Ouch!"
Heard after expensive, breakable object meets one or more of child's toes before shattering. (Compare *"Oops!"*: Heard after expensive, breakable object meets floor only.)

overnight camp
Beaver goes away. Beavis comes back.

overprotective
Dad wears two condoms.

overscheduled
Child's day resembles the viewing grid in *TV Guide*.

P

pacifier

The thing that babies love to throw farthest. In the Olympics of life, this activity rivals the shot put. Unlike the shot put, though, pacifiers tend to become lost and collect wadded up dust balls when thrown.

parent

Someone to hand the empty wrappers to.

parent chaperone

An adult who looks conspicuously old.

parent support group
Blue Cross/Blue Shield.

parenthood
An odyssey, the objective of which is the safe delivery of children into adulthood, whereupon parent, like the noble salmon, may die.

parenting books
The book world's way of telling parents they've got no instincts.

parents with teenage driver
Crash test dummies.

parent-teacher conference
Where day staff and night staff meet to compare notes.

pass-fail
System of grading in which child merely needs to display minimal brain wave pattern.

paternity suit
Dad's work clothes.

pediatrician
A children's doctor who treats anxious parents along with their kids.

peekaboo

Parent pretends he can't see child. A mini-vacation.

peer pressure

Thirty kids in a Honda.

percentiles

Where child falls in relation to the total population of kids her age with respect to height and weight. Charted by pediatrician during WELL VISIT. The source of playground dispute as children stand back-to-back and claim, "Bigger," which is somehow related to "better."

permission slip
When kids forget to ask first.

pet names
Those that child outgrows hearing but parent doesn't outgrow saying.

PG-rated
What an eight-year-old calls babyish.

picky eater
A kid with an overweight dog.

picture books

Prepare child for *Playboy*.

pierced ears

The emblem of modern androgyny. A mall activity.

pimples

Fair trade for parent's wrinkles.

Pierced Ears

play date

Where two or more children gather for a period
of mutual recreation. Generally includes
bopping each other on the head with G.I. Joes
or other play matter. The conclusion of the play
date occurs when one or more child raises a
welt.

play group

A block party.

Play-Doh

Stuff that sticks to dogs.

playground

The scene of many an accident. Stay clear of the monkey bars unless you're within walking distance of a hospital.

playing favorites

Parent plays oldies.

playing hooky

Child redefining number of days in school year.

playing house

Can you say *rising property taxes*?

Playground

poor sport

A bad activity for child, such as football.

postpartum depression

The realization that real life has begun, which is always depressing.

power struggle

In the ultimate struggle for power, kids would be king. To do battle, parent must remember who holds the deed to the house and pays out the allowance.

precocious

Four years old going on forty.

pregnancy
Gain plus pain.

pregnancy test
An exam that is graded on a curve.

pre-K
A through *J*.

preschool
Where kids first learn to separate, engaging in such touching good-byes as molding themselves to parents' ankles.

presoaking
Child jumps in puddles on way home.

preverbal
Stage at which child communicates with piercing screams that parent must interpret.

principal
School CEO.

private school
Where notes sent home are usually bills.

prom

Night fabled for losing virginity.

promise

What child makes when *his* end of the deal
seems far away.

PTA meeting

Group therapy.

pull toy

Mom's earrings.

Q

quality time

What you're having when you're not with the kids.

quiet time

That period of the day when child stores up energy so she may attack anew.

R

radio-controlled

Child with Walkman.

rattle
Anything that baby shakes that annoys you.

readiness
What parent displays outside bathroom occupied by teenager doing hair.

rec room
Any room kids have just been in.

recital
Forced appreciation of child's talent.

Recital

rectal thermometer

Temperature-taking device that acts like a missile when expelled from the body of an unwilling child.

relatives

People who think they know more about baby than you.

remote control

What parents have over their kids—once their kids are out the door.

retainer

What sits on dinner table beside teenager's plate.

role model

A patterning device. Child finds someone as distasteful to parent as humanly possible, then likens himself to him.

Rollerblading

The only time kids are in-line.

R-rated

Those movies child watches with the baby-sitter.

Rollerblading

S

school
Parent's recess.

school band
Where all play to their own drummer.

school bus driver
Frustrated amusement ride operator.

school cafeteria
Where mom's lunch gets traded.

School Bus Driver

school dress code
What everybody else is wearing.

school locker
Kid's messy room at school.

school night
Any evening when the good TV shows are on late.

school nurse
Person who must determine whether child's stomach cramps are real or faked.

school play
The Sound of Music Man of La Mancha.

school records
An account of child's academic and behavioral performance. Also available on CD.

school registration
Learner's permit.

school store
Student shopping network.

schoolbooks

When they should be at home, they're at school—and vice versa.

schoolboy crush

Kid at the bottom of a heap.

science fair

Kids receive ribbons for things their parents made.

seat belt

That which straps in precious cargo. Child may complain about wearing—but its use is nonnegotiable.

second childhood

"Hey, Daddy, those are *my* trains!"

security blanket

That dragged, sucked on, sweated into piece of cloth that will fray, grow smaller, and eventually disintegrate, but not before leaving a lasting impression. Like *Citizen Kane*'s Rosebud, your child will never forget Blanky.

self-sufficient

Child able to do for self—allowing parent more time for general worrying.

Security Blanket

separation anxiety

Fear of losing TV privileges.

sharing

A concept children understand as it applies to parent's things—not theirs.

show-and-tell

The public display of your intimate apparel to all of your child's classmates.

sibling

Person used to deflect blame, as in "Mom, *he* did it!"

Sibling

sick visit
Kid with unnamed rash comes over.

single parent
One whose job description calls for two.

sired
Fathered by. Mothered is *mired*.

slang
Words that become obsolete the moment a parent utters them.

127

sleeping bag

Kid crepe.

sleeping through night

What parent must relearn once baby gets the hang of it.

sleepovers

Parent obliges to have child's friend spend night. This turns into longest experience of parent next to birth of child.

sleepwalking

How parent of newborn gets through day. It
helps if there are rubber pads on walls and
furniture, as parent will continually collide with
these surfaces and become black-and-blue.

snow days

Jubilation for child, juggling for working parent
who must supply coverage at home and at
office. A forward-looking solution to problem is
cloning of parent.

snowsuit

Kid's diuretic. As soon as suit goes on, nature
calls.

Snow Days

Snugli

Pouch that allows child to spit up on you as you bond.

"Some assembly required"

Words that belong on a warning label.

sonogram

Baby's first photo opportunity.

spoiled brat

Says more about parent than about child.

sports equipment

Items that decorate house.

stain-resistant

Spot that won't come out.

stepparent

Another adult who lives in the house that kids won't listen to.

storage space

That which gets eaten up by child's stuff, while your things systematically find their way to the street.

strained carrots
The orange stuff on kitchen wall.

stretch marks
When child gets an F—but says he got a B.

stroller
Vehicle which enables child to rest and recharge her batteries while parent pushes and sweats. One more example of how poorly designed life is.

student council

An introduction to political reality in which the election of candidates is based on popularity rather than merit.

study habits

Child positioned in front of TV with snacks and telephone. Books and writing material optional.

sugar high

Child defying gravity.

summa cum laude

Latin for "My parents will be getting me a car."

summer job

That which son takes to meet babes.

Sunday best

Clothes that get muddy faster than regular clothes.

suspension

Child has three days off to play Game Boy.

sweet 16

Cinderella rite of passage, marked by driver's permit and skin eruptions.

T

tamper-resistant

Kid can get into it; parent cannot.

teacher

Somebody your kids think they know more than.

tee ball

Living proof that you can't hit a stationary object with a piece of wood.

teenager

Person with chronic PMS.

teething biscuit

Orange cookie that will wind up at the bottom of the hamper affixed to parent's favorite white shirt.

telephone

Thing kids answer with, "Yeah, who is it?"

temporary tattoos

Those that wash off after three baths or three months, whichever comes sooner.

term paper

What kid lets go to last minute, and then has you type—and it's *your* fault when he gets only a B.

terrible twos

This term applies to any age that has two digits, particularly, but not exclusively, the teen years, and includes two-digit months as well. Children from the ages of 0 to 9 months generally excluded on the sole basis that they are single-digit entities and have not yet gathered enough momentum.

3 A.M. feeding

That which interrupts parent's two minutes of sleep.

thumb sucking

Early oral fixation later replaced by smoking and overeating.

time-out chair

Spot in which child reflects on her misbehavior. Removed from desired stimuli, child may rejoin larger social setting upon ring of egg timer and delivery of apology properly made. Parent may insist on notarized apology, done in triplicate, with a copy sent to state capital.

toilet training

A process of elimination.

tooth fairy

Remember when twenty-five cents took care of a regular tooth, maybe fifty cents for a molar? It costs more these days. Have your Visa or MasterCard ready.

toy chest

Empty bin surrounded by toys.

toys

Items your child will beg for at holiday time and then lose interest in almost immediately.

tracking

An educational term for ability grouping, this is, in reality, the unmistakable appearance of mud through your kitchen.

training bra

Tiny piece of spandex a ten-year-old thinks will transform her from a flat-chested fifth-grader to a full-figured Guess? girl.

tree house

Real estate for kids only.

triplets

A mini-series.

Tracking

tutor
Person paid to teach child what he missed
during his fifth-period nap.

TV violence
Fighting over who watches what.

twenty-something
The cost of a sitter for Saturday night.

U

"Uh-huh"
Child affirmative.

Training Bra

"Uh-uh"
Child refusing peas.

umbilical cord
This highly functioning conduit connects parent to child more effectively than MCI. Cut but not severed at birth.

V

valedictorian
Black belt in brains.

Video Games

Velcro

Kids' shoelaces.

video games

Brain-deadening activity enjoyed by millions of children. Once engaged, they won't see or hear you until the quarters run out. If video system is installed at home, child may forget all bodily functions. A narcotic for the '90s.

video store

Parent wanting Disney; child wanting *Blood and Guts, Part 4.*

W

"Waaaaaaaahhhh!!"
Child holding note longer than Streisand.

walker
Infant bumper car.

well visit
Previously called "checkup," if for no other reason than you go and write a check.

working mother
This term is redundant redundant.

Working Mother

X

"XXX & OOO" (kisses and hugs)
Kid currency.

Y

yo-yo
The only thing in the house that will walk the dog.

Z

Zen baby

Baby contemplating navel.

zillion

The number of excuses kids have.

zoo

Natural habitat for the lion (dad), bear (mamma), and piggies (guess who).